Other ways to earn money from home + How to collect the money generated? + How much money can you earn online? + How to earn money fast and easy?

TABLE OF CONTENTS

Make money online safely is already a reality. The network of networks is an ocean full of opportunities to get extra money every month from the comfort of your home. Like thousands of people, I have done it and you can do it too. Seriously, don't hesitate for a moment

Even so, as in any job in real life, you have to dedicate time and effort, nobody here gives anything away. Whoever thinks that he is going to get a lot of money fast reading this blog, let him forget about it. We are not going that way here.

My name is Robert and in this book I want to share with you the different ways that I use to earn money online from home in this year 2021. What started as a simple hobby a few years ago, today has become my main source of income. income, even above my job. Something surprising and that I never imagined.

It is likely that if you have come this far it is because you want to achieve exactly the same thing, right? Live in a more comfortable and independent way, without bosses, with flexible hours and doing what you really like. Or maybe your goals are more modest and you are simply looking to generate extra income every month.

In either case, I think my experience can be very helpful, especially to avoid making certain beginner mistakes, knowing how to make money on the Internet legally and being up to date with the best opportunities available today. How about? Shall we start? ?

Is it real that making money online?

Yes, of course it is real. It is common for people who are beginning to be interested in this world of online business, do not believe that they can really start to earn real money. Distrust is logical.

To demonstrate the opposite, in Dinerobits I will show the payment vouchers that I am receiving from the different sites that I use on a personal level and that you will be able to see in each of the articles dedicated to each business.

In addition to serving as proof, the receipts of the different payments that I am receiving I believe can serve as an exceptional source of motivation, especially for all those people who are interested in Internet business but need a little "push" to start .

Without going any further, in my beginnings what most motivated me to continue working were the payment vouchers that I saw on the Internet (in forums, blogs, etc.), some of which seemed impossible to me to get.

As time has passed, I have realized that nothing is impossible and that when you put all your effort into something, you can achieve incredible things. It is something you will see when you see some of my income.

Can anyone earn money from home?

Without any doubt yes, but the majority fail in the attempt. Why? Well, it is always for the same reason: lack of patience and perseverance, two mandatory virtues in this world. Principles in business are always tough, both in real life (offline) and on the Internet.

At the beginning you start earning very little (you really add up from penny to penny), but as you learn and dedicate more time, you begin to see results and add up in dollars and euros.

But unlike when you open a normal business (I know what I'm talking about, I have one), on the Internet you can start from scratch, without having a penny, without asking anyone for money, without any investment and above, from the comfort of your home and without any schedule or obligation.

Some common questions that many people ask are the following:

Do you have to be of a certain age?

Not at all. Although there are some pages that only allow people of legal age to register, 95% of the sites that you will see on this blog are for people of any age and condition. Namely:

- **Retired** looking to earn extra money to supplement their pension.
- **Young people** Y teenagers who want to get an income in a simple way to be able to pay for their expenses and / or whims.
- **Normal people** who cannot find work and who seek to earn a living on the Internet.
- **Workers** looking to earn additional money to supplement their salary.

Can you make money on the Internet from any country?

Yes. Most of the pages you'll see on this blog are for users from all countries. Anyway, in the description of each site you will have an exact description in this regard.

Is it necessary to have a credit card?

No. Almost all of the sites where we work are completely free and will pay us through electronic processors such as PayPal, Skrill, Payoneer, Neteller, AirTM, bank transfer, and so on. It's as easy as opening an account in each of them (it's free) and we'll be ready to receive our earnings.

So, if you are a persistent person, with patience, you like the Internet and you want to start earning money online in a staggered, reliable and serious way, you are in the right place ?

How to get money on the Internet? What I need?

Starting to earn money from home does not require any type of investment or initial outlay, however, you will need some essential "tools".

* ?A computer. It can be desktop or portable, it is completely indifferent. It does not matter if it is old or has few benefits. Internet businesses hardly consume resources at the hardware level. A mobile phone or tablet can also work.

- ?An internet connection. This is obvious, right??

- ✉ An email. Although anyone can be worth it, from my experience I can tell you that it is best to use one from Gmail.

- ?An account with at least one payment processor. It is best to have several in your portfolio to take advantage of the potential of all the pages. In the help section (in the upper right part of the blog), you will find all the ones that I use. A little later I will talk about the most important ones.

- ?Desire to work As I said at the beginning, making money online is not an easy task, so, at the very least, you will have to dedicate some time and effort to it.

How to make money online: The 33 most reliable methods

In the blog you will find many pages to start earning free money on the Internet. The variety is immense and you will surely find one that suits your tastes and / or needs.?

As you will see, almost all the sites and pages we use today are to earn money without investing, which will always give us additional security.

So that you don't get lost, we have organized them all into 31 different categories, which will increase as we discover or use other forms or methods.

They are as follows:

1.- Permissive email marketing emails

In these companies we will earn money by opening advertising emails that will reach us by email. These emails usually lead to other pages with all kinds of offers and promotions, although the only condition to receive our reward will be to open said emails, without cheating or cardboard?

It is a simple and free way to add extra money. We will only use serious and reliable sites that pay on time. The way to receive the money will almost always be through processors like PayPal, Skrill and bank transfer.

2.- Paid online surveys

On these pages we will earn money by filling out surveys and giving our opinion about products, brands and services. We will only use free sites that do not require any type of payment or subscription.

Without a doubt, making money with online surveys is one of the best ways to get an extra salary on a monthly basis, so this type of page should not be missing in your online business portfolio. The most famous of all isySense.

The minimum amounts to be able to charge are usually quite small, so that anyone wanting to work can reach them with relative ease. The usual payment method on these pages is usually PayPal.

3.- Paid advertising and PTC sites

Pages where you simply have to click on ads to earn money. In most cases, it will be worth clicking on them, you won't even have to see them.

It is one of the most popular and widespread methods to earn money on the Internet, so the variety of sites of this style is immense. In addition, its use is extremely simple and suitable for anyone. The most famous of all isNeoBux.

Another advantage of these types of sites to earn money by watching advertising is that they serve users from all countries, so, wherever you are from, you can register and start earning income easily and for free from the first moment ?

4.- Savings and cashback system

Pages in which we will save and earn money with our usual purchases on the Internet. For each purchase made, they will return a percentage of it.

They also have other very interesting ways to earn free money such as viewing videos, registering on other pages, exclusive offers, and so on.

If you are that type of person who loves to save, do not hesitate to take a look at these types of pages. The most famous of all isBeRuby

5.- Online investments

We will analyze places where we can get very good returns for our savings with the least possible risk. Our two fundamental guidelines in these types of sites will always be prudence and diversification.

To do this, we will use the money that we generate in the rest of the free pages whenever possible, which will make our pocketbook practically not affected in any case.

In any case, these types of pages will in no case account for more than 5% of our online business portfolio. As I said at the beginning, our main goal is to make money online without investing.

6.- Promotion pages and social networks

Social networks today are one of the best ways to earn money online for free. In addition to generating income, these sites will allow you to get followers and increase your social presence. This aspect is essential to grow in your projects and online businesses.

There are many platforms that are looking for influencers with a good number of followers to promote all kinds of campaigns. In return, you will receive an economic remuneration practically without doing anything. Very interesting!

7.- Make money playing for free

Different pages that will allow us to win gifts, prizes and money just for playing for free. In this section we will also include free sites where we can win real money betting on our favorite sports without risking a single euro.

Earning extra money while having a good time sounds good, huh? Well, it's completely real. As I said at the beginning, the Internet offers incredible opportunities?

8.- Applications for mobile devices

Free apps to earn money comfortably with our mobile phone. It is one of the easiest ways to generate extra money from anywhere. Also, if you are looking to earn money quickly (although in small amounts) and without any complications, it is a method that you will love.

There are apps for both Android and iOS devices. As a general rule, the rewards are usually cash through PayPal and gift vouchers to buy on Amazon.

9.- Affiliate platforms

Affiliate platforms where we can promote dozens of products, companies and services on our websites or blogs and get good commissions. If you manage to have a website with a lot of traffic, the profits can be huge.

Regardless of the theme of your site, do not hesitate to take a look at these types of platforms, since you will surely find something from which you can get an economic return. Making money with blogs or web pages has never been easier.

10.- Freelance work from home

The online communities for the sale of small services is one of the best opportunities that exist today for all those who seek to work from home in what they like the most and are good at.

On these platforms, a multitude of services can be offered from $ 5, so if you are an expert in some type of subject, here you will find the best solution to make yourself known and earn an extra salary from the comfort of your home. .

11.- Online sale of photographs

If you like photography and on top of that you want to earn extra money with it, on the Internet you will find multiple platforms where you can do it. Free sites that will facilitate the entire process of uploading, displaying and selling your photos.

If you have a wide and good quality photo catalog, it can be a great opportunity to show your talent and who knows whether to make the leap to professionalism. In addition, once uploaded, the photos become a source of passive income where you will not have to do anything else.

12.- Youtube and other video platforms

The most famous online video platform in the world has become a real gold mine. Thousands of people are already making money with their YouTube channel, in which their job consists of uploading videos that are then monetized through advertising from partners such as Adsense, Machinima, TGN, etc.

Any theme is conducive to creating a channel and being successful with it, although there are some that are especially ideal for this sector, such as video games and / or humor. YouTube has become a platform where anyone, young or old, can earn extra money and even make a living from it.

Making money with YouTube has become a real profession, so, if you have ever considered it, now is the time ?

13.- Sale of electronic books

The purchase of electronic books has become an unstoppable phenomenon that is gradually relegating reading on paper to the background. Whether you are an amateur writer or a veteran, the Internet can be the great opportunity you were looking for to make yourself known and perhaps make a living from it.

The possibilities are immense and the steps to get started much simpler than in conventional literature. Feel free to take a look at our basic tips to get you started on making money writing.

14.- Make money with a blog

A blog is the best tool to start making money on the Internet, there is no doubt about that. A blog will allow you to express your ideas and knowledge to the rest of the world, with all that that entails. Through it, you can let others know what pages you work with, your results in them, what products and / or resources you use, and so on. This has enormous potential.

By working honestly and sincerely, you can create a community of followers who will read your content and trust you, and that is invaluable. A successful blog can become a true passive income generating machine regardless of its topic: cooking, sports, health, games, travel, technology, making money online, etc.

Choose a topic that you are passionate about and that you can write about and contribute things of value to others and create a blog, you will not regret it. You can have a professional blog up and running for little money and in return you can get thousands of euros if you work with perseverance, discipline and dedication. It is not an easy road, but nothing in life (if you work honestly) is.

If you are looking for how to get money in a safe and stable, do not hesitate and make a blog as soon as possible. Start making money with a blog now?

15.- Bitcoin and other virtual currencies

Bitcoin is a cryptocurrency that is completely revolutionizing the world of currencies. Its value is constantly growing and more and more sites are accepting it as a payment and collection method.

For a few years, the number of pages where we can get small fractions of this virtual currency has been growing dramatically.

Considering that these sites are completely free of charge and available to users in all countries, it is a great opportunity to earn free money on the Internet with relative ease.

As if this were not enough, if the trend in its price continues to rise as in recent years, we could find spectacular revaluations in the not too distant future. Without a doubt, a great opportunity ?

16.- Buy and sell web domains

One of the oldest ways to earn money online is to buy and sell domains, both new and old. There are many strategies in this regard. One of them is based on finding domains that are below their real value and then selling them much more expensive.

Another method (although much more difficult) is based on buying a domain and making it grow until it reaches a value that is well above the money and time invested in it.

It is obvious that to apply this strategy it is necessary to have knowledge of SEO and web positioning, but today this is available to everyone thanks to the immense information that is on the net?

The most used platform to buy and sell domains is Sedo.

17.- Become an influencer

If there is a social network that has grown enormously in recent years, that is Instagram. Millions of people around the world upload huge amounts of images and photos sharing their life, their work, their hobbies, and so on.

This has not gone unnoticed by the big brands, who have set their eyes on this social network as the ideal platform to carry out their advertising campaigns. And there is no better way to do them than through well-known faces and with great influence among their followers, known as "influencers".

Therefore, being an influencer on Instagram can become one of the best ways to make money with the Internet.

18.- Online sale through dropshipping

Dropshipping is a form of entrepreneurship that is allowing thousands of people to earn money from home with their own online business. The great advantage of this system is the possibility of having a huge catalog of products for sale without having to physically have them.

This supposes a brutal saving in costs, since it is not necessary to have products in stock or a physical space (shop, commercial premises, warehouse, etc). The business basically consists of acting as an intermediary between the customers and the final supplier (for example, Amazon).

Therefore, the only function (in addition to creating the web), will be to pass the orders to the supplier so that he takes care of everything: shipping, packaging, warranty, etc. Without any doubt, dropshipping is one of the best ideas to earn money that exist on the net?

19.- Trading and investments with cryptocurrencies

For lovers of strong emotions and speculative trading, one of the best ways to get money online is the cryptocurrency market. The enormous volatility of these virtual currencies has made them a real gold mine for anyone who knows how to move with judgment and cold blood. Companies like Binance are a clear example.

Anyway, before embarking on the world of trading with cryptocurrencies, it is essential to acquire some basic knowledge, since, just as you can earn a lot of money, can also be lost just as easily.

Another fundamental aspect is choosing a trustworthy platform where all operations can be carried out with rigor and security. One of the best known is eToro, a veteran broker with many years behind him where to invest and trade with Bitcoin, Ethereum and many other cryptocurrencies and that is available to anyone.

And is that thanks to the social trading system, we can base our strategy on simply copying other more expert and experienced traders to do the work for us ?

20.- Earn money creating your own product

One of the best ways to get money today is by creating your own digital product, commonly known as an info product. One of the great advantages of this system is that, regardless of the theme to which you dedicate yourself, you can always create a product that adapts to what people are looking for and demanding in the digital age.

Also, although creating a (quality) info-product takes a lot of time and work, it can become the best way to passively earn money online. That is why more and more bloggers, influencers and all kinds of freelancers are making the leap to creating their own digital products.

If you think you have mastered any subject and can provide quality information to others, do not hesitate and translate your knowledge into your own info product. You will not regret!

21.- Sports bets and welcome bonuses

Bookmakers have become one of the great businesses of the 21st century. That is why the number of these types of sites grows exponentially year after year. At Dinerobits we are not in favor of abusing these types of pages, since if they are not used wisely they can make us lose a lot of money.

However, we are in favor of taking advantage of the succulent welcome bonuses offered by this type of platform as a claim to attract new customers. With a good strategy and a serious and rigorous working method (such as the one proposed in NinjaBet), you can get great benefits with little risk.

The same goes for gambling and casino sites. They are not a good alternative to earn money at home in a safe and stable way (in the long term, of course), but you can take advantage of the bonuses and special welcome offers.

A good example of this are pages like Botemania or Sportium, where the benefit / risk equation is quite positive for us?

22.- Writing and writing articles

Are you good at writing? Do you have the facility to write content on any subject? If so, you have a great opportunity to make money from home online with relative ease. Due to the exponential increase in website creation, the search for content writers is increasing.

There are many people who are dedicated to creating and positioning blogs and web pages, but then they need to "fill" those sites with useful and original content for their readers. This is where the editors come into play, who are the people who are in charge of writing the articles that will shape all those sites.

For this reason, many blogs, web pages and even newspapers, need the services of people who simply have the gift of writing well, or what is the same, having a large vocabulary and of course a good spelling.

The easiest way to qualify for this type of income is to use platforms that connect editors and website owners such as Fiverr, TextMaster, Freelancer, etc. All are valid for users in Spain and Latin America.

Another way is simply by directly contacting blogs, websites, or newspapers. In all of them you will find a contact section where you can offer your services. You will be surprised at the amount of positive responses?.

23.- Binary options

Binary options are one of the most fashionable ways to generate money today. Its operation is based on guessing if the price of a financial asset goes up or down, it's that simple. The problem is that what seems so easy, it really is not. Great knowledge of technical and fundamental analysis and great psychology are needed for high risk trading.

Just as big profits can be made, losses can also be just as large. You have to be disciplined, have a good strategy, and draw up a thorough trading plan to be successful in such a volatile and speculative market.

24.- Tasks, mini-jobs and crowdsourcing

There are many pages that offer the possibility of earning money by performing small tasks and mini jobs online. It is one of the most reliable methods that exist on the net to earn dollars and / or euros easily and for free. Best of all, the variety of tasks to be carried out is immense, so if there is something you don't like or are not good at, you have many more to choose from.

Examples? Take photos of a certain subject, record videos, try games, download applications, listen to music, translate texts, write articles, categorize images and… much more! All these types of mini-jobs are included in two types of pages: Get Paid To (GPT) and crowdsourcing.

Both one and the other stand out for the possibility of getting money without the need for referrals. Work and individual effort is what makes the difference when it comes to achieving great results?

25.- Other methods to generate money

Here we will include many other methods to earn money on the Internet (or as my Argentine friends say, earn money online) such as: installation of programs, surf bars, earn money for surfing, automatic systems, and so on.

The number of ways to earn dollars online and generate money from home is increasing day by day?

26.- Help other bloggers like you

If you have achieved some success with your blog, such as having thousands of visits a day, you can take the opportunity to take advantage of that "fame" and show other people how you have achieved it.

A very effective way is through the creation of an electronic book, where you can collect the information of your most successful articles and add additional and relevant information, such as your SEO strategies to receive more traffic.

Another option widely used today is through personalized advice, where through programs such as Hangouts or Skype, you can maintain direct contact (even with a webcam) with those people or companies that request your services.

Finally, there is also the possibility of giving talks at specialized conferences, such as in universities or education centers. If you have a good public speaking, this method can bring you big income?

27.- Work from home translating texts

Did you know that more than 60% of the content that is generated on the Internet today is in English? Incredible true? In the same way, many of the creators who write in the language of Shakespeare seek to expand their content in other borders, especially in Spain and Latin America.

For this reason, the demand for people who are fluent in English and who are willing to translate texts into Spanish is enormous today. A unique opportunity to earn money from home without too much difficulty (not without work).

The companies that request these services are usually foreign (obviously), such as WorldLingo Andovar or Translator's Cafe. There are also educational platforms where you can acquire all the knowledge and tools necessary to start Work from home doing translations.

Subsequently, these platforms are responsible for putting you in contact with other companies that are looking for this type of translation services, thus causing a very interesting mutual benefit.

28.- Earn money solving captchas

Who has not solved a captcha ever? Those distorted letters or symbols that only humans can solve and that serve to prevent the use of robots and other fraudulent automation that swarm the Internet.

As robots are getting smarter, it is necessary to perfect this system to do it every time safer . For this, there are companies that pay money to anyone who is willing to solve captchas from their computer screen. Some examples of this type of platform areKolotibablo Y 2Captcha.

Honestly, it is quite a heavy and monotonous job, not suitable for all types of people. Still, it is one of the simplest and safest ways to earn money online, since it is a real and sustainable business.

29.- Earn money shortening links

Link shorteners were born with the aim of simplifying those URLs that are so long that we sometimes want to share on our social networks and that, due to lack of space, sometimes do not fit. As time has passed, this tool has become an interesting way to get money, both for users and for companies.

The operation is very simple: once a link is shortened, it will look smaller and therefore easier to share. In addition to that, it will contain a small advertising format that can be skipped within seconds of clicking on it.

Thanks to this, companies can easily advertise any type of product and / or service and the person who shared the link will earn money every time someone clicks on it. Simple right??

Although there are many platforms of this style, the most famous and recommended is the great Ad.fly.

30.- Get free Amazon gift cards

This method of making money at home is booming. It is about getting checks, cards and gift codes to buy for free in the most famous online store in the world: Amazon.

Did you know that there are many pages that pay their users through this system? Instead of charging through traditional methods (PayPal, Skrill, bank transfer, etc.), there is also the option of redeeming your rewards through cards and gift vouchers.

How useful is this? If you are a regular buyer in this online store, you will get your orders much cheaper and even… free! Interesting, right? This is an amazing way to save that I particularly like quite a bit?

31.- Work as a virtual assistant

It is a proven fact that the Internet has radically changed the way thousands of people around the world work. This is especially evident in some professions such as clerks, teachers, computer scientists and secretaries, although there are many more.

The reason for this is obvious: the tasks that are carried out in this type of work can be done online without the need for physical presence. Thus, many companies give their employees the opportunity to perform their functions without having to travel to the office.

This offers multiple benefits to the worker, such as saving time and money when traveling or a better way to reconcile family life. Also, experienced virtual assistants can charge up to $ 50 per hour.

32.- Sell characters and video game skills

I have discovered this method recently and it seems absolutely brutal, especially if you are a video game fan like me. If you are not very into this world it may seem like something a bit geek, but the point is that it is real and it is possible to get a lot of money.

It is about selling advanced game accounts with their characters, abilities, magic, weapons, powers, and so on. For example, a friend of mine recently sold his Fortnite account for almost $ 100. What have you done after? Another has been created to level it up and sell it again. How about??

In countries with great economic difficulties this method has become very popular, since you simply have to spend the whole day playing to later sell your achievements within the game in question. On sites like playerauctions.com you will find a large community of players willing to buy and sell everything.

33.- Create and sell plugins for WordPress

Do you have programming knowledge? And if not, do you know someone who has them and who can form a team with you? Either one way or another, you can take advantage of the incredible market niche that WordPress plugins represent (the

CMS with which most websites are built today). It is a real gold mine!?

Plugins are small programs that add all kinds of functionality to a blog or website. There are thousands of them and they cover all kinds of needs: security, SEO, social interactions, form creation, web design, spam filters, compliance with laws, performance and speed, and so on.

Personally, I don't know of any blog that doesn't make use of at least four or five of these programs. They make your life a lot easier and also provide your website with features that are currently absolutely essential. In short, they are a must for every webmaster.

The method that works best for plugin creators is the "Freemium" format, that is, free versions with basic features and a Premium version with more professional features. Without going any further, in this blog I use three paid plugins with an annual subscription and they are very worth it.

The key in this sector is to find a need for users and create a tool (or improve existing ones) that provides the best solution. For example, in recent times some entrepreneurs have been (literally) lined with the creation of plugins that allow them to comply with the new cookie law at the European level.

Other ways to earn money from home

Although this blog is especially focused on Internet businesses, we cannot ignore that there are also many opportunities to generate income from home that do not always need an Internet connection.

1.- Make money with crafts

Are you good at crafts? Well, it can be a great opportunity for you. In such a globalized world, sometimes things made by hand and with a point of personalization of their own are missed. Without going any further, my wife earns good extra money every month thanks to the sale of Amigurumis, dolls made with crochet using crochet techniques.

Another curious case is that of the father of a great friend of mine. After retiring, he has devoted himself to his great passion: painting pictures. Well, look where, he is starting to sell them because it looks very good and people are demanding it. Besides enjoying like a dwarf, he is complementing his pension wonderfully?

Other examples could be: making bags, accessories, cushions, patterns, T-shirts, jewelry, ornaments, key chains, toys, etc. Imagination to the power!

2.- He teaches private classes

Do you master a specific topic? It can be anything: languages, computers, music, crafts, electricity, etc. Well, it may be the perfect time to teach others and in return receive financial compensation.

To get started, all you need is a bit of publicity to make yourself known. You can do it through online platforms such as Milanuncios or directly go out and use word of mouth.

If you are really good at some subject and you also have a talent for teaching, sooner or later people will look for you and not the other way around ?

3.- Take care of other people's children

Due to the new social and economic reality, it is a fact that when both parents work, they have very little time to care for and care for their children. That is where people who are unemployed or have a lot of free time can take advantage of to earn extra money.

Without going any further, one of my best friends has found in this task almost a semi-profession, since she dedicates much of the day to it. He is a well-known person in the town for his patience and a special gift for children.

Thus, he has become the trusted person for many parents who are burdened by work or who need to disconnect for a while for whatever reason. He has gone from being unemployed to making money doing what he likes best.

All he did at first was advertise on an Internet ad page and spread the word around homes, bars, and shops. The rest has come by itself?

4.- Sell the clothes that you no longer use

Have you ever considered selling all those clothes that for whatever reason you never wear? Did you know that you can get some good extra money very easily? Currently there are quite a few platforms that have made the sale of used clothing a quick and safe process.

On the other hand, this activity encourages caring for the environment and responsible consumption, since it is a proven fact that in Western countries much more clothes are bought than necessary (which entails a brutal waste of natural resources such as water) .

As if all this were not enough, getting rid of all the clothes that you no longer wear will make you gain a lot of space in your closets, something that on a personal level has come to me from pearls because I had them to burst ?

If you are curious about this topic and want to take your first steps, I invite you to read my article on how and where **sell used clothes**. There you will find everything you need to know about this interesting way to save and get money along with the most recommended platforms and applications.

How are we going to collect the money generated on the Internet?

This is one of the most frequent questions that I usually receive on the blog. It is normal that everyone wants to know why the media is going to receive the profits that it generates in all the pages that exist to make money on the Internet.

This is where the famous payment processors, also known as e-wallets, come into play. These sites are neither more nor less than small (or not so small) virtual banks where we can receive all the money that we generate in the network.

Afterwards, we will have the possibility to send the accumulated funds to our bank, credit card, etc. Having a well diversified portfolio of electronic wallets, we will have no problem when it comes to receiving our money and later disposing of it for the use we want to give it.

The most famous of these payment processors is PayPal, that surely many of you will already know. It is undoubtedly the best known and most used, so it is the first that we all should have. Opening an account is very easy and of course completely free.

In any case, if we want to really take advantage of this to earn money on the Internet, it is essential to have several electronic wallets, since many pages do not have PayPal as a payment method.

In addition, the differences between some processors and others can sometimes be very large, both in the conditions of use, as in the options available and the applicable commissions.

Therefore, the key is to diversify

For this reason, it is important to have a good range of possibilities to later be able to decide where it is best for us to have our income generated on the Internet.

Next I will show you the **online banks without commissions**and the major e-wallets that I have been using for several years. Of course, all comply with current legislation, are regulated and are totally reliable.

PayPal

The most widely used and well-known payment processor in the world with more than 227 million users spread across the globe. Although its strong point is the ability to buy in thousands of online stores, you can also send and receive payments safely and transfer the funds to your bank account. 100% recommended (not to say essential).

N26

Online bank account without commissions and with multiple advantages. Free MasterCard card, free ATM withdrawals, mobile app and guarantee fund from Germany. Also, you can link with PayPal and withdraw funds from this payment processor with your card. One last!

Skrill

Formerly known as MoneyBookers, this electronic wallet has been a reference in the world of betting and online casinos for many years. It has all the legal and security requirements and has lower commissions than the competition. It has a debit card and the possibility of sending money to the bank account.

Coinbase

The best wallet to receive our payments in bitcoins. Possibility to buy and sell this cryptocurrency and then exchange it for euros or dollars to transfer them to our bank account.

Bit2me

One of the best electronic cryptocurrency wallets in the world. It belongs to a Spanish company of recognized prestige and with several international awards. Very low commissions and excellent support. It has its own network of physical points of sale (Tikebit), which allows you to obtain digital currencies without using credit cards or banks.

Neteller

Another highly reputable payment processor with a long history. Ideal for withdrawing money at ATMs thanks to your debit card. Widely used in the world of Forex and online games.

Binance
One of the most prestigious cryptocurrency exchanges in the
world. Many supported currencies and very low commissions. Its
growth in recent years has been incredible and it has tools that
the competition does not have: loan system, staking, P2P buying
and selling, futures contracts, its own cryptocurrency (BNB) and
several more ...

AirTM
The definitive platform to solve the problem with currency
exchange. In addition to serving as a wallet, we can change any
payment received in dollars or euros to our local currency. Ideal
for countries that suffer from currency problems like Venezuela.

Lots of variety to earn money online

All the pages that you will see in each category work individually.
The ideal is to be registered in all that we can, since although we
will not win large amounts in any, the sum of all of them can be
very interesting at the end of the month?

Not everything is making money in this life, it is essential to be
comfortable with what we do, therefore, I recommend that you
review well all the pages and categories that we have on the
blog. I am sure that you will like some and others you will not: it is
a matter of choosing the ones that really seem interesting to you.

This blog is focused on the Spanish and Latin American public,
so you will not have any problem when registering in most of the
sites that we propose. There are some pages that only serve
Spanish, but it is something that you have indicated in the review
of each page.

As you will see as you become familiar with online businesses, one of the most important aspects is the issue of the referrals.

What are referrals?

Referrals are those people who register on the different pages to earn money on the Internet through your recommendation or link. Once registered, they will become part of your network and they are the ones that will allow you to increase your income exponentially.

Of course, by being referred by someone you will not lose absolutely anything, you will earn your money 100%, but the person who recommended you will take a commission (which will be different on each page)..

In online businesses, getting referrals and / or affiliates is extremely important and that is why it is increasingly complicated: the competition is enormous.

For this reason, at Dinerobits we will be compiling ways to get the maximum possible referrals along with another point that is often forgotten: taking care of those referrals with all the help you can give them (something crucial so that they remain motivated and wanting to continue earning money In Internet).

The importance of teamwork

And it is that although at first it may not seem like it, this is teamwork, where the key is to help each other. Some do it one way and others another. For example, my way of helping is by having updated information on all the pages that I propose on the blog.

In addition to that, I try to answer all the comments and emails that I receive, since I think that is the least I should do when a person has registered under a link of mine and needs my help.

I also like to motivate my readers and referrals through contests and sweepstakes that I run from time to time. Is it a simple way to thank the support of people who read the blog and / or follow me on social networks?

So you know, whether or not you are my referral, I will be happy to help you in any way I can. Of course, if you have knowledge of sites where you can earn money online seriously and constantly, do not hesitate to **contact me.**

How much money can you earn online?

The eternal question that everyone asks when they start in this world (and that you will also be asking yourself right now), is: how much money can I earn? A lot of? Little? The answer is very difficult to answer, especially since it is something that will depend exclusively on you.

How many hours do you plan to dedicate to Internet business? 2 hours a day? 10 hours a day? As I said at the beginning, nobody here gives anything away and only those who work with perseverance and dedication will see important results. Fast (and honest) money doesn't exist.

There are people who take this of making money online without investing as a simple hobby, dedicating little time (1 hour a day maximum), and with the simple objective of getting a little extra money to spend it on some other whim.

On the contrary, there are people who seek to earn money on the Internet "for real", with the firm purpose of achieving financial freedom through what are known as passive income, the great goal of every online entrepreneur.

Obviously, to achieve that goal it is not worth spending an hour a day in front of the computer, right? Or is it that you know of a job where he earns a buck working one hour a day? I suppose that like me, you will not know any, otherwise you would not be reading this, right??

Effort + patience = positive results

Therefore the reflection is simple: if you want to earn a lot of money, you will have to work a lot and very hard, especially at the beginning. Without going any further, I started dedicating about 8-10 hours a day during the first year.

Create this blog, learn the working mechanism of all the pages, research on the Internet about this world, read many **financial education books**and personal finances, learn a bit of SEO to position my articles, create profiles on all social networks, and so on. I barely slept 4 or 5 hours a day.

As time has passed (since August 2013), experience has allowed me to reduce the time I dedicate to certain things. I remember that at the beginning, I could spend two hours watching all the PTC's advertisements, which now only takes me half an hour.

Doing a simple survey was a real hell, and now I am able to do them two by two in different browser tabs ?Don't worry, it's something that will happen to you too. At first you will see everything "super difficult", and little by little you will realize how simple it is.

But one thing is that it is not complicated, and quite another is that you do not have to dedicate many hours if you want to earn money on the Internet for real. I know several people who have made Internet businesses their daily job and earn real salaries.

In my personal case, I dedicate about 4-6 hours a day to this, which is the maximum that my free time allows me. Yes, you read that right, my free time. And I am a freelancer with a normal and ordinary job, and I do this to earn money on the Internet from home to complement my salary and because I like it.

Even so, there have been some months in which I have earned more than $ 2,000 with the pages to earn money online for free that I have indicated above, imagine if I dedicated myself full time! ?

The potential of the Internet is almost unlimited, and only It depends on you how far can you go ?

How to earn easy money online?

I don't want you to be fooled. In this blog you will not find miraculous ways to become a millionaire, among things because they do not exist. I only know the way of hard work and daily effort. I don't like shortcuts or shenanigans to make money overnight. Earning money online is possible, but not easy.

In DineroBits you will not see recommendations to invest large sums of money either. 90% of the pages you will see on this blog are completely free now and forever. In those that require investment, I will always recommend the same: maximum prudence.

Never invest money that you need to live, it is a very serious mistake that many people make. My recommendation is that you do like me, and only invest a small percentage of the profits that you will get from all the free sites that I will be showing you, but if possible, never touch your pocket?